D1057678

THE PREDICTIONS LIBRARY

TAROT

David V. Barrett

DORLING KINDERSLEY
London · New York · Stuttgart

A DORLING KINDERSLEY BOOK

Senior Editor • Sharon Lucas
Art Editor • Anna Benjamin
Managing Editor • Krystyna Mayer
Managing Art Editor • Derek Coombes
DTP Designer • Cressida Joyce
Production Controller • Sarah Fuller
US Editor • Connie Mersel

First American Edition, 1995
2 4 6 8 10 9 7 5 3 1

Published in the United States by Dorling Kindersley Publishing, Inc.,
95 Madison Avenue, New York, New York 10016

Distributed by Houghton Mifflin Company, Boston.

Library of Congress Cataloging-in-Publication Data

Barrett, David V.
  Tarot / by David V. Barrett. -- 1st American ed.
    p.   cm. -- (The predictions library)
  ISBN 0-7894-0306-4
  1. Tarot.   I. Title.   II. Series: Barrett, David V.   Predictions
library.
BF1879.T2B374   1995
133 . 3'2424--dc20   95-12890
                                                      CIP

Reproduced by East Anglian Engraving, Norwich
Printed and bound in Hong Kong by Imago

CONTENTS

INTRODUCING
TAROT

TAROT IS PROBABLY THE MOST POPULAR FORM OF
DIVINATION IN THE WORLD. THERE ARE MANY
DIFFERENT TAROT PACKS, AND EVERYONE SHOULD BE
ABLE TO FIND AT LEAST ONE TO SUIT THEIR TASTE.

Tarot enjoys its popularity for a variety of reasons – partly because the cards are extremely beautiful objects to hold and examine, partly because the images on the cards "speak" deeply to most users, and partly because it can provide remarkably clear and relevant readings.

With a few exceptions, Tarot packs contain 78 cards – the Major Arcana (22 cards) and the Minor Arcana (56 cards). Unique to Tarot packs are the 22 cards of the Major Arcana. Their symbolic images are often beautiful and colorful, and lie at the very heart of Tarot. The powerful archetypes illustrated on these cards are a product of the Western Mystery Tradition, but are recognizable in most

THE SUN
This Sun card is from the Visconti-Sforza Tarot. The oldest pack in existence, it dates from around 1450.

cultures. They include the Fool, the seeker after truth; the Emperor, the figure of male authority; and the Moon, symbolic of both intuition and deception. The Fool is the only Major Arcana card to appear in the ordinary pack of playing cards, where it is the Joker.

~ ⊙ ~

The Minor Arcana is considered to be the ancestor of the ordinary pack of playing cards. It contains four suits – Cups (Hearts), Wands, Staves, or Batons (Clubs), Coins, Pentacles, or Disks (Diamonds), and Swords (Spades), plus four extra cards. Each suit contains ten Number cards and four Court cards – King, Queen, Knight, and Page.

~ ⊙ ~

The Major and Minor Arcana, used either separately or together, can provide great insight into yourself and other people.

They can also be an aid to psychological awareness and spiritual development, and act as a guide and teacher along your pathway of life.

~ ⊙ ~

Some people treat Tarot casually, and others treat it with reverence. This book takes a respectful approach. Remember that other people might see Tarot differently from you, and never pick up someone else's pack without asking them first.

THE TWO OF CUPS
Although this Two of Cups from the Visconti-Sforza Tarot pack is highly ornate, it simply shows the number of symbols of the suit.

HISTORY
of TAROT

ALTHOUGH TAROT IS UNDOUBTEDLY OLD, IT IS NOT
ANCIENT. THERE HAVE BEEN SEVERAL INFLUENTIAL
CLAIMS THAT TAROT IS THOUSANDS OF YEARS OLD,
BUT ITS ORIGINS WERE AROUND 500 YEARS AGO.

Tarot is believed to have originated in late 14th- or early 15th-century Italy. This is because the images of the Major Arcana bear some similarity to early engravings of a series of 14th-century Italian poems, "The Triumphs of Petrarch." These poems are about the triumph of love, chastity, death, fame, time, and eternity. They are moral allegories about human life and the state of the soul, and seem to share certain similarities with Tarot. The Italian card game *Tarocco* contains 22 cards similar to the Major Arcana, which are known as triumphs or trumps.

It is also possible that the Major Arcana was devised as a striking pictorial reminder for spiritually aware but

FORTUNE-TELLING PACKS
Many 19th-century fortune-telling packs showed scenes from daily life – this card from a French pack of the 1820s, Épitre aux Dames, *shows a country house.*

semiliterate people, in much the same way as stained glass windows in churches remind congregations of Bible stories. Although some religious critics have denounced Tarot as merely "the Devil's Picture Book," much of the symbolism is Christian in origin.

Many authorities have claimed a much older history. In 1781, Antoine Court de Gebelin published his own Tarot pack and claimed that the Major Arcana was an ancient Egyptian book containing secret, magical wisdom.

A Paris barber and wigmaker, Alliette, took up Gebelin's ideas. Under the reversed name Etteilla, he wrote books on occult philosophy, established himself as a high society fortune-teller, and published his own Tarot packs. These were different from Gebelin's pack, which had been far closer to traditional designs, but like many authorities on Tarot, Etteilla claimed that his own pack restored the original Egyptian designs. He called Tarot the "Book of Thoth" after the Egyptian god of magic, writing, medicine, and secret wisdom.

The fascination with all things Egyptian has survived, and many packs still contain

PARLOR GAMES
These cards from the French pack Le Jeu du Destin Antique *are more suited to parlor games than the serious inquiry of Tarot.*

Egyptian imagery. As late as 1944, Aleister Crowley added further weight to the Egyptian theory by naming his own Tarot deck the "Book of Thoth."

EARLY CARDS

ALTHOUGH TAROT IS 500 YEARS OLD, MOST OF THE
ESOTERIC INTERPRETATIONS TEND TO COME FROM
FRENCH AND BRITISH OCCULTISTS LIVING BETWEEN
THE LATE 18TH AND EARLY 20TH CENTURIES.

The French occultist Etteilla was fascinated by the links between Tarot and the Kabbalah, a Jewish esoteric system that absorbed some aspects of Christianity and Islam in the 14th to 16th centuries. The Kabbalah uses a complex diagrammatic system to illustrate the relationship between God and man – ten points on the Tree of Life are joined by 22 paths, labeled with the 22 letters of the Hebrew alphabet. Etteilla's ideas were expanded further by Eliphas Lévi and Papus, who worked out correspondences between the 22 paths of the Tree of Life and the 22 cards of the Major Arcana.

The British occult society, the Hermetic Order of the Golden Dawn, made Tarot

FLEMISH TAROT
This Hermit is from an 18th-century Flemish pack. It is similar in tradition to the Marseille Tarot.

4. 3.ᵉ El. 2.ᵉ Cré.

DÉPOUILLEMENT.

69

AIR.

FROM STAR TO AIR
*In the Grand Etteilla, many cards
are renamed. For example, the Star
is known in this pack as Air.*

than the Major Arcana.
Many Tarot packs have
drawn directly from the
Golden Dawn meanings,
including the Rider-Waite,
Aleister Crowley's Book of
Thoth, and the Morgan-
Greer Tarot. All these packs
stem from the same root, but
their images and symbolism
are often markedly different
from each other.

13

correspond with the
Kabbalah more closely by
placing the Fool before
Card 1 instead of before
Card 21, and swapping
Justice and Fortitude, Cards
8 and 11. It also codified
the meanings of the Minor
Arcana, in line with its own
esoteric teachings. Until this
time, the Minor Arcana had
been of much less importance

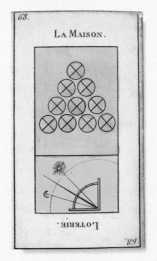

68.

LA MAISON.

LOTERIE.

89

TEN OF PENTACLES
*The Grand Etteilla's Ten of Pentacles
represents the home (La Maison); the
reversed meaning is chance (Loterie).*

TYPES *of* PACK

A WIDE VARIETY OF TAROT PACKS ARE USED, BUT
PERHAPS THE BEST-KNOWN AND MOST POPULAR ARE
TWO TRADITIONAL EUROPEAN PACKS, THE MARSEILLE
AND THE SWISS IJJ, AS WELL AS THE EARLY 20TH-
CENTURY RIDER-WAITE PACK.

MARSEILLE
*The Marseille is a traditional French design. These two
cards, the Ten of Pentacles and the Tower, are taken
from an early 18th-century pack. Some of these
designs still appear almost unaltered
in many modern packs.*

RIDER-WAITE

The Rider-Waite pack was designed by the esotericist A. E. Waite, and was first published by Rider & Co. in 1910. Waite was a leading member of the Order of the Golden Dawn, and his pack embodies some of the Order's secret teaching. Many of the packs of recent years have followed Waite's symbolism. The Rider-Waite was the first deck to have pictorial Minor Arcana cards, which illustrate the meanings assigned to the cards.

SWISS IJJ

The Swiss IJJ pack is a traditional late 18th- or early 19th-century pack, in which the Pope and Papess (or High Priestess) are replaced by the Greek gods Jupiter and Juno, giving the pack the letters JJ. During the "Age of Reason" following the French Revolution, many of the religious aspects of the Major Arcana cards were toned down, and the Pope and Papess in particular were often replaced by other characters.

UNUSUAL PACKS

THERE ARE RADICALLY DIFFERENT INTERPRETATIONS
OF TAROT. THESE UNUSUAL PACKS TEND TO BE BASED
ON MYTHOLOGY, A PARTICULAR PHILOSOPHY, OR A
SPECIAL ENTHUSIASM OF THE DESIGNER.

ELEMENTAL TAROT
*This 1988 pack uses the elements of Earth, Fire, Air, and
Water for the four suits of the Minor Arcana, plus the
esoteric fifth element, Spirit, for the Major Arcana.*

MOTHERPEACE TAROT

The roundness of the Motherpeace Tarot (1981) emphasizes the Moon, the Mother, and the circularity of life. It is a feminist spiritual interpretation, and its images mainly portray goddesses and female magic.

SARDINIA TAROT

Osvaldo Menegazzi's Sardinia pack (1984) uses bronze statues to illustrate an aspect of the meaning of each Major Arcana card. Strands of coral, used by Sardinians for magic and healing, surround each statue.

DIVINATORY HANDS AND SHELLS

These small but beautifully striking Major Arcana images are from Menegazzi's Le Mani Divinatorie (1979) and Le Conchiglie Divinatorie (1975).

TAROT
& DIVINATION

TAROT IS PARTICULARLY WELL SUITED TO DIVINING
AND DISCOVERING YOUR PERSONALITY AND PROBLEMS.
TAROT'S SYMBOLIC IMAGES ENHANCE YOUR INTUITION
AND CAN SUGGEST POSSIBLE PATHS TO FOLLOW.

Tarot can reach deep into the question that you are asking. By mixing the structured and the random, it can reveal the sort of person you are – your strengths and weaknesses, abilities and difficulties.

DEATH
The Kashmir Tarot (1984) shows Death holding a sword and an hourglass in the midst of continuous creative energy. Instead of plummeting to destruction, the boat and its human passengers rise up to new life.

Tarot can identify the immediate question, show the path that you are most likely to follow, and consider how outside influences, people, and circumstances could affect your options. It can identify possible obstacles and dangers and show the best road to success.

Although Tarot is a very powerful divining tool, it cannot reveal specifics. However, it can suggest solutions to problems and show the factors that may help or hinder you. The choice is always yours – you can follow Tarot's guidance, or choose to ignore it.

Father of Wands in the East
King of Wands

KING OF WANDS

The Court cards of the individualistic Haindl Tarot (1988) draw upon the mythology of many lands. Usually the King of Wands signifies a good communicator and negotiator, and a fatherly, generous mediator. However, in a pack as individual as this, it is necessary for the Tarot reader to consider carefully the choice of mythological character, here the Hindu deity Brahma, in order to appreciate fully the deep nuances and layers of meaning in each card.

THE HERMIT

Several cards from the Frown Strong Tarot (1991) use imagery that is considerably different from the usual, which changes the meanings of the cards from the generally accepted sense. The Frown Strong's Hermit has taken on some of the attributes of the Fool, with the dog snapping at his heels. This card speaks of the need to focus on one clear idea and follow it, rather than be so confused and unperceptive that a lantern is needed in broad daylight.

9

OTHER USES
of TAROT

TAROT CAN BE USED FOR MANY PURPOSES OTHER THAN
DIVINATION. TRY USING TAROT FOR EXTREMELY DEEP
PERSONAL STUDY, AS A FOCUS FOR MEDITATION, OR AS
A FRAMEWORK FOR STORYTELLING.

Tarot's imagery and its links with esoteric systems make it ideal for use in many rituals.

Tarot can be helpful for meditation – simply choose a card and fix your mind on it. If you have a choice to make, study the Lovers and consider whether to follow your head or your heart. Or if you wish to heal someone, choose the card that represents them, and hold it in your mind while you focus on Temperance.

Six of Hearts

SIX OF HEARTS
The Inner Child deck (1992) uses images from fairy stories and mythology. Winged Hearts represent Cups, and the Six of Cups includes the idea of friendship. This card shows a mermaid, riding a stork – a bringer of new life. The mermaid helps her friends rise up from the sea.

Tarot's imagery can also be used to provide a framework for storytelling – sometimes storytellers use Tarot cards to create characters and situations for their work.

DEATH AND THE HERMIT

The Wonderland deck (1989) uses scenes from Lewis Carroll's books Alice's Adventures in Wonderland *(1865) and* Through the Looking Glass *(1872) to illustrate the meanings of the cards. Death shows the Queen of Hearts shouting "Off with his head!" and the Hermit shows the dormouse withdrawing into a teapot from the bustle of life.*

EIGHT AND NINE OF WANDS

The Mythic Tarot is based on Greek mythology – the Major Arcana cards feature many gods and heroes, while each of the four suits relates one of the famous stories of Greek mythology. The suit of Wands shows Jason in his quest for the Golden Fleece. The Eight of Wands, which denotes successful progress towards a desired goal, shows the sure, swift passage of his ship, the Argo. The Nine of Wands, which denotes strength and steely determination, illustrates the safe passage of the Argo between the Clashing Islands at the entrance to the Euxine Sea.

EIGHT OF WANDS

NINE OF WANDS

THE MAJOR ARCANA

THE 22 CARDS OF THE MAJOR ARCANA SYMBOLIZE VERY POWERFUL ARCHETYPES OF PEOPLE, VIRTUES, SPIRITUAL STATES, AND CIRCUMSTANCES.

The Major Arcana is at the heart of Tarot. The 22 cards represent the range of human life – physical, intellectual, emotional, and spiritual. They illustrate your strengths and weaknesses, hopes and fears, the most godly parts of your personality, and the darkest parts of yourself.

Some cards might reveal unwelcome truths – you may need to make a self-sacrifice (the Hanged Man), allow a part of your life to die in order that new life can begin (Death), or throw off the chains that bind you to selfish behavior (the Devil). Other cards show joy, hope, healing, or victory.

Many of the Major Arcana cards show an archetype – a figure who represents the entire essence of a type of person. Archetypes include the warm, nurturing mother figure; the strong, firm authority figure; the traditional, formal religious leader; or the mystical, mysterious, magical person. An archetype might represent a real person, a part of yourself, or an abstract symbol in your life.

Each Major Arcana card contains both positive and negative forces – one person's firmness can be another's rigidity, and one person's poetic vision can be another's foolish dream. For example, the crashing Tower can mean a fresh start. This does not depend on which way up a card is, but on your question, the reader's interpretation, the card's position, and the interplay between each and every other card in the spread.

0 — THE FOOL

THE FOOL
The Fool represents an innocent setting out on a journey. He is naively ignorant of what might face him on the way, is stepping into the unknown, and might, as in many packs, be about to step off a high cliff into great danger. The other cards of the Major Arcana will warn, guide, and help him along his way.

DOG CAN BE A FAITHFUL COMPANION, BUT USUALLY REPRESENTS LIFE'S TROUBLES SNAPPING AT THE FOOL'S HEELS

LEMNISCATE IS THE SIGN OF INFINITY

I — THE MAGICIAN

23

THE MAGICIAN
The Magician controls and coordinates events. He holds and pulls many strings at once. He can be a manipulator and even a trickster. This is a card of communication, of powerful teaching and guidance, and a link between God and humans, Heaven and Earth, and spirit and matter.

PACK *Morgan-Greer Tarot*
PUBLISHED *1979*
ARTIST *Bill Greer, directed by Lloyd Morgan*

THE HIGH PRIESTESS

The High Priestess, or Papess, denotes esoteric spiritual knowledge. She is usually shown as a mysterious, magical woman, and is often partly hidden. She is closely linked to the Moon and can therefore represent deception as well as truth.

B AND J ARE BOAZ AND JACHIN, NAMES ON THE PILLARS IN SOLOMON'S TEMPLE IN ANCIENT JERUSALEM

SCROLL OF THE SACRED TORAH, THE BOOK OF LAW IN JEWISH SCRIPTURE, SYMBOLIZING HIDDEN WISDOM

THE HIGH PRIESTESS

24

THE EMPRESS.

THE EMPRESS

The Empress symbolizes the Earth Mother, fertility, fecundity, fruitfulness, and natural growth. She is the homemaker, and she embodies nurturing motherhood as well as sensual sexuality. She can also represent self-indulgence and female domination.

VENUS SYMBOL INDICATES FEMALE SEXUALITY

CORN SYMBOLIZES NATURAL FRUITFULNESS

THE EMPEROR

The Emperor embodies authority, solidity, stability, and the firm rule of law. He denotes a sense of responsibility and control, including self-control. He can be firm but fair or exercise total inflexibility and male domination.

EMPEROR SITS ON SOLID, FOUR-SQUARE THRONE OF LAW

THE EMPEROR.

TRIPLE TIARA IS A TRADITIONAL SIGN OF THE POPE

THE HIEROPHANT

25

THE HIGH PRIEST

The High Priest, or Pope, represents religious orthodoxy. He is the mediator between Earth and Heaven, and denotes spiritual wisdom. He shows the security of firm belief, but he can also imply strict adherence to a hierarchical tradition and a reluctance to explore new spiritual paths.

 PACK *Rider-Waite*
PUBLISHED *1910, reissued 1971*
ARTIST *Pamela Colman-Smith, directed by A. E. Waite*

THE LOVERS

This card is also known as the Lover. Surprisingly, it has less to do with romantic love than with the choice faced if you love two or more people, or two or more incompatible things, equally. It symbolizes that a choice has to be made, perhaps between the spiritual and the sensual, or between intuition and reason.

PARIS HAS TO CHOOSE BETWEEN POWER, RICHES, LOVE, GLORY, AND HONOR

WHITE AND BLACK HORSES SYMBOLIZE THE CONSCIOUS AND THE UNCONSCIOUS

26

THE CHARIOT

In many Tarot packs the Chariot is pulled by two horses or sphinxes, which willfully try to pull in different directions. The Chariot symbolizes life and the need for firm control, in order to stay on a straight path and keep opposing forces in balance.

PACK *Mythic Tarot*
PUBLISHED *1989*
ARTIST *Tricia Newell, directed by Juliet Sharman-Burke and Liz Greene*

JUSTICE

JUSTICE

This card denotes the impartial administration of justice – careful weighing of both sides of a case, balancing innocence and guilt, right and wrong, light and dark, then reaching and accepting the correct decision. It might not be the decision that you want, and Justice can sometimes show that you are in the wrong.

SCALES AND SWORD ARE TRADITIONAL SYMBOLS OF JUSTICE

27

THE HERMIT

THE HERMIT

The Hermit signifies a period of withdrawal from the hectic pace of life to study, contemplate, and meditate. It symbolizes renewal – physical, mental, and especially spiritual, as well as the ability to return with new wisdom to face and overcome old problems.

LAMP LIGHTS THE WAY FOR THE HERMIT AND HIS FOLLOWERS

THE WHEEL OF FORTUNE

The Wheel of Fortune emphasizes the circle of the seasons and the cycle of life. There is no failure, only delay. Without change there is stagnation and often it is necessary to go down in order to come up again. The card indicates that you should not be defeated by your problems – face them as challenges, and incorporate them in the turning wheel of your life.

THE WHEEL OF FORTUNE

DESCENDING SNAKE AND RISING FOX REPRESENT DESCENT INTO DEATH, THEN ASCENT INTO REBIRTH

28

STRENGTH

FORTITUDE

This card symbolizes strength – not just brute physical strength, but also strength of will and intention. Fortitude implies staying power, and the determination to keep going until you achieve a satisfactory result. True strength is a virtue that can overcome seemingly impossible problems through calmness, skillfulness, and firmness of intent.

LION REPRESENTS STRONG INSTINCTIVE DESIRES, WHICH NEED TO BE FIRMLY TAMED

THE HANGED MAN

This card shows that self-sacrifice might be necessary in order to attain freedom and transformation. It can also mean that you should look at your problem from a different angle. In Norse legend, Odin hung upside down from the World Tree for nine days and nights in a self-sacrifice to gain knowledge of the mystical runes.

HANGED MAN IS SERENE AND CALM
DESPITE THE ROPES THAT BIND HIM

BEARDED FACE
SUGGESTS APPARENT
FEROCITY OF DEATH

THE HANGED MAN

DEATH

DEATH

Death signifies transition. It is not the end, but the beginning of a new life on a higher plane. However, new life cannot start until the old life is dead. For example, it is difficult to let go of a relationship, job, or home, but it may be necessary in order to make a fresh start on a new life.

PACK *Ukiyoe*
PUBLISHED *1983*
ARTIST *Koji Foruta, under supervision of Stuart R. Kaplan*

TEMPERANCE

This card symbolizes wholeness, harmony, and healing. It indicates that instead of reacting too quickly and emotionally to events, you should show temperance, moderation, and patience. Justice should be balanced with mercy, and action with contemplation. Show some compassion – if you are whole within yourself, you will be able to help and heal others.

ANGEL SHOWS BALANCE BETWEEN THE CONSCIOUS AND THE UNCONSCIOUS

DEVIL SYMBOLIZES BONDAGE TO SELFISHNESS

30

THE DEVIL

The Tarot Devil symbolizes bondage, not necessarily to evil, but to selfishness, arrogance, and pride. It suggests that it is up to you to break these self-inflicted bonds in order to be free – if you do not, you will remain trapped, and be held back from spiritual, emotional, and physical advancement.

PACK *Celtic Tarot*
PUBLISHED *1990*
ARTIST *Manuel Gonzales Miranda*

LA·MAISON·DIEU

THE TOWER

Sometimes called the House of God, the Tower represents unexpected upheavals and reversals. It illustrates the sudden intervention of fate in our lives, which can turn everything upside down. It is not necessarily catastrophic and could be an opportunity for an enforced fresh start. The Tower can also represent the rigidity of long-held false beliefs and habits, which may need to be completely changed.

LIGHTNING SYMBOLIZES THE SUDDEN INTERVENTION OF FATE

L'ÉTOILE

THE STAR

The Star is a shining light in the darkness – the card of hope, faith, and inspiration, as well as renewal and replenishment. Water is poured from two jugs onto both land and pool, symbolizing the conscious and the unconscious. The land is refreshed and the pool replenished. This card is the human outcome of the angel's harmony and healing shown by the Temperance card.

WATER REPRESENTS THE UNCONSCIOUS OR THE SPIRITUAL; LAND REPRESENTS THE CONSCIOUS OR THE MATERIAL

THE MOON

The Moon is the card of lovers and poets, of intuition and madness, and of hidden depths and deception. It contains both light and darkness, esoteric spirituality and confusion. It creates dreams and visions, but these may be fantasies. Nothing can be depended upon because everything is touched in some way by the absence of reason or sanity.

CRAYFISH SYMBOLIZES THE DARK FORCES OF THE UNCONSCIOUSNESS, WHICH MUST BE GUARDED AGAINST

32

THE SUN

The Sun represents joy, success, and fulfillment. It symbolizes the warmth and light that sustains life on Earth, and new opportunities – the Sun rising in the morning heralds a new day, full of potential. The card also represents family joy and hope in the future.

CHILDREN REPRESENT A RETURN TO INNOCENCE AND THE OPPORTUNITY FOR A FRESH START

JUDGMENT

Sometimes called the Angel, this card usually shows a man, woman, and child – often naked – being called from their graves by an angel's trumpet blast. It symbolizes readiness for rebirth by judging ourselves and evaluating our past efforts and achievements with honesty. It incorporates summing up our lives, accounting and atoning for our faults, and giving and accepting forgiveness.

MAN, LION, BULL AND EAGLE SYMBOLIZE MATTHEW, MARK, LUKE AND JOHN

PEOPLE REPRESENT SPIRITUAL REBIRTH

33

THE WORLD

The World is the card of completion, attainment, and success. The Fool has reached the end of his journey and is now to be crowned with the laurel wreath of victory. This may symbolize material success, but it also implies self-knowledge, spiritual understanding and maturity, and a oneness with the universe.

PACK *Marseille*
PUBLISHED *1701–15*
ARTIST *Jean Dodal*

THE MINOR ARCANA

THE 56 CARDS OF THE MINOR ARCANA REPRESENT THE
PEOPLE, CONDITIONS, AND SITUATIONS IN YOUR
EVERYDAY LIFE. THERE ARE FOUR SUITS – CUPS, WANDS
(ALSO KNOWN AS BATONS OR CLUBS), COINS (ALSO
KNOWN AS PENTACLES), AND SWORDS.

COURT CARDS

Unlike the normal pack of
playing cards, there are four
Court cards in each suit of
the Minor Arcana – King,
Queen, Knight, and Page.
These cards may represent
people in your life, such as
a dominating father or
employer, a loving mother or
girlfriend, an intelligent and
ambitious young person, or a
child – or they may represent
these qualities in yourself.

A King card might symbolize
the masculine aspects of a
female personality – her
animus, and a Queen card
might symbolize the feminine
aspects of a male personality –
his *anima*.

Although the Court cards
usually represent people, they
might sometimes symbolize

the concepts of, for example,
domination, ambition,
impatience, faithfulness,
caring, or the love of new
ideas. During a Tarot
reading, when deciding to
whom or to what the Court
cards refer, always be guided
by the context of the other
cards in the spread and by
your own intuition.

NUMBER CARDS

There are ten Number cards
in each suit of the Minor
Arcana. They show various
situations in your life, such
as pain, frustration, and
persecution, or cooperation,
communication, and
perseverance. These can be
defined as failure or success.

Although different Tarot
packs emphasize a variety of
meanings, the ten Number

ACE OF WANDS
Based on a classic Tarot design from 1736, this Ace of Wands is from the Spanish Tarot.

cards of each suit of the Minor Arcana tend to symbolize the following:

ACE: the essence of the suit, signifying new beginnings;
TWO: opposites, balance or conflict, and duality;
THREE: growth, fruitfulness, results, and action;
FOUR: stability, solidity, organization, and logic;

FIVE: mutability, change, and some uncertainty;
SIX: natural balance, peace, and harmony;
SEVEN: the end of one phase, and progress to the next;
EIGHT: the balancing of opposing forces;
NINE: the force and nature of the suit;
TEN: completion.

ACE OF CUPS
This Ace of Cups, showing a simple chalice, is from the Tarot of the Witches (1973).

35

ACE OF CUPS

CUPS

THE SUIT OF CUPS IS CONNECTED WITH EMOTIONS,
PASSIONS, AND SPIRITUALITY, AND IS LINKED WITH THE
ELEMENT OF WATER.

COURT CARDS

The divinatory meanings of the court cards are:

KING: a good negotiator, maybe a professional person, interested in the arts and sciences; often concealing or perhaps not fully in touch with his own feelings;

QUEEN: a warm, gentle woman, both sensuous and sensitive, intuitive, and spiritually deep with an air of mystery, but who may seem too dreamy, "other worldly," and unrealistic;

KNIGHT: a sensitive person, who is romantically questing for truth, but who is possibly not very practical and may be too easily influenced; new opportunities;

PAGE: a kind young person, quiet and studious, perhaps with artistic or psychic abilities; the time for quiet contemplation and exploring new feelings.

NUMBER CARDS

The divinatory meanings of the number cards are:

ACE: the essence of water; spiritual and emotional

KING OF CUPS

This Ukiyoe Tarot card shows the King holding a lacquer cup, which depicts a water scene.

KING OF CUPS

nourishment, and perhaps
a new relationship;
TWO: friendship and an
increase in cooperation;
THREE: peace and happiness;
the outcome of loving union;
FOUR: emotional stagnation,
dissatisfaction, and apathy;
FIVE: disappointment, loss,
and regret, but there is hope;
SIX: happy memories lead to
present comfort, but this
can be pointless nostalgia;
SEVEN: too many choices,
and some might just be

fantasies; choose well from
among the illusions;
EIGHT: rejection of a much-
loved past in order to move on;
NINE: physical and emotional
stability; fulfillment of a
desire, and sharing;
TEN: completion, family love,
contentment, and the safety
of the home.

TWO AND THREE OF CUPS

The Two of Cups is from the Español or Spanish Tarot, and the Three of Cups is from the Morgan-Greer Tarot.

WANDS

THE SUIT OF WANDS IS CONNECTED WITH ENERGY AND
AMBITION, HARD WORK AND PROGRESS, AND IT IS
LINKED WITH THE ELEMENT OF FIRE.

COURT CARDS
The divinatory meanings of
the court cards are:
KING: a charming, witty, and
generous person, who is
honest, conscientious, and
just, but can be impatient
with detail, and autocratic;

QUEEN: a friendly, generous,
and caring person who is also
practical, an excellent
businesswoman, capable,
independent-minded, and
naturally authoritative;
KNIGHT: a well-liked,
generous person, confident
and energetic, who is full of
interesting ideas and actions,
but who can be unpredictable;
PAGE: a lively, reliable young
person who is a trusted
messenger, and who carries
unusual or good news.

NUMBER CARDS
The divinatory meanings of
the number cards are:
ACE: the essence of fire;
creativity, enthusiasm, and
ambition, with an exciting
new project or career;

PAGE OF WANDS

PAGE OF WANDS
*The Mythic Tarot's Page of
Wands is Phryxus. He is a
character from Greek mythology.*

TWO: a firm leader with strength of will and high ideals who must now make important decisions;
THREE: the practical expression of these plans, which are moving ahead;
FOUR: achievement, the results of this hard work, with continued growth;
FIVE: unavoidable problems and various small and petty annoyances, which must be met by some skill;

THREE AND FOUR OF WANDS
The Three of Wands is from Le Tarot de Marseille, *and the Four of Wands is from the Russian Tarot.*

39

SIX: a success, achievement, and considerable public recognition of hard work;
SEVEN: opposition, a challenge that you must overcome through skill, courage, strength of will, and a determination to succeed;
EIGHT: a sudden rapid movement and swift progress to success, but beware of hastily made decisions;
NINE: strength and determination are needed whatever the opposition;
TEN: success has become a burden and a trap.

COINS

THE SUIT OF COINS IS CONNECTED WITH THE
MATERIAL WORLD, SUCH AS MONEY AND PRACTICAL
MATTERS. IT IS LINKED WITH THE ELEMENT OF EARTH.

COURT CARDS

The divinatory meanings of
the court cards are:
KING: a dependable and loyal
leader, not very imaginative
or intelligent, who is always
content with himself and
with his life;
QUEEN: a practical and
capable businesswoman, who
is generous, but enjoys her
comfort, prosperity, and
social prestige too much;
KNIGHT: a reliable and
patient person, but may be
too stolid and conventional;
PAGE: a hardworking,
meticulous, discerning young
person who will become a
good administrator, but can
be too diligent and serious.

NUMBER CARDS

The divinatory meanings of
the number cards are:
ACE: the essence of earth;
financial security, material
comfort, physical well-being,
and a sense of inner worth;
TWO: as a result of vast
change and fluctuations,
you must be adaptable, and

KNIGHT OF COINS

This Chevalier de Denier, *the
Knight of Coins, is from an early
18th-century Marseille Tarot.*

CAVALIER EL DENIER

balance the many variables with considerable skill;

THREE: your skillful work is appreciated and rewarded; from this start, further success can be achieved;

FOUR: material security, but this can easily lead to greed and stagnation;

FIVE: impoverishment and loss of security, but help may be available if you pay attention to detail and do not despair;

SIX: generosity and using your good fortune and success to benefit others, clear debts, and repay outstanding favors;

SEVEN: don't rest on your past efforts or be complacent, since success will only come from continued hard work;

EIGHT: turning your personal interests, enthusiasms, and skills to profitable and satisfying ends;

NINE: accomplishment, and the enjoyment of the hard-earned success of your personal achievements;

TEN: security and wealth, including emotional wealth with the support and stability of family and home.

TWO AND FIVE OF COINS

The Two of Coins is from the Mini-Motherpeace Round Tarot, and the Five is from the Ukiyoe Tarot.

41

SWORDS

THE SUIT OF SWORDS IS CONNECTED WITH THE MIND,
ACTIVITY, AND FORCE. IT IS LINKED WITH THE
ELEMENT AIR. HOWEVER, THE SWORD IS TWO-EDGED.

COURT CARDS
The divinatory meanings of
the court cards are:
KING: a strong upholder of
law, order, and authority
who exercises power,
command, and judgment;
although he likes new ideas,
he can be very domineering,
hard, and cruel;
QUEEN: an intelligent, self-
reliant person, who is skilled
at achieving her will, but she
may have known sorrow;
KNIGHT: a courageous and
skillful warrior, clever and
ambitious, impatient for
action, and who will defeat
opposition ruthlessly;
PAGE: an alert, quick-minded,
perceptive young person
who is clever, but possibly
deceitful, and would make a
good emissary or spy.

NUMBER CARDS
The divinatory meanings of
the number cards are:
ACE: the essence of air;
power and justice through
strength and determination;

QUEEN OF SWORDS

QUEEN OF SWORDS
*This card is from the Morgan-
Greer Tarot. It represents strength,
independence, and determination.*

TWO: a stalemate or an
uneasy equilibrium;
THREE: an absence,
separation, or painful loss,
but new hope lies ahead;
FOUR: physical rest as a
respite from trouble, and
perhaps a spiritual retreat;
FIVE: dishonor, ruined plans,
and a need to accept defeat –

NINE AND TWO OF SWORDS

The Nine of Swords is from the Rider-Waite Tarot, and the Two of Swords is from El Gran Tarot Esoterico.

try to swallow your pride,
and move on;
SIX: the overcoming of an
obstacle, a move away from
present difficulties, and a
possible journey;
SEVEN: use logic, clear
thinking, and even cunning
to overcome opposition;
EIGHT: you feel restricted
and helpless, but patience,
courage, and attention to
detail will see you through;
NINE: misery and despair, but
the fear is worse than the
reality, and dwelling on it
will invariably make it worse;
TEN: ruin, pain, and absolute
desolation, after which your
life can only improve.

43

READING
THE TAROT

ALLOW THE IMAGES ON THE CARDS TO "SPEAK" TO
YOUR SUBCONSCIOUS MIND. IF YOUR IMAGINATION
FLOWS, YOUR INTERPRETATION SHOULD BE ACCURATE
BECAUSE IT WILL BE GUIDED BY YOUR INTUITION.

Some Tarot readers keep their cards carefully wrapped in a square of black silk inside a handmade wooden box on a shelf above head height. They may also play soft music, light a candle, and burn incense during a reading.

~ ⁇ ~

All of these activities can be useful if they help you to create an atmosphere, but they are not essential. The most important aspects when reading Tarot are a respect for the ideas illustrated on the cards and a serious approach to the reading.

~ ⁇ ~

First you must decide which type of spread is most useful for the question you intend to ask. Calm your mind, cut out all distractions, and keep the question clear in your

head. Shuffle the cards, then cut them in three piles. Put the piles back together and deal off the cards to be used in the reading one at a time, face downward, with each in its correct position. It is unnecessary to use reversed cards – each card of the Major Arcana has a range of meanings, and there are both positive and negative cards in the Minor Arcana.

~ ⁇ ~

In all spreads, each position has its own meaning. Turn over each card in order, one at a time, bearing in mind the question, the meaning of the card, the meaning of its position, and how it relates to the other cards in the spread. Consider how these factors interrelate, then turn over the next card and do the same. When all the cards are showing, see if there is an overall feeling to the spread such as a predominance of Major Arcana cards, one suit, or Court cards, or a feeling of joy, frustration, success, or danger.

Look through the cards again, see the story that they tell together, and apply this to the question and the questioner (also known as the querent).

Always allow your intuition to be guided by the cards and try to draw a lesson from the spread. It is vital that the querent remains fully involved in the reading – asking and answering questions – rather than being merely a passive observer.

When the reading is over, take some time to do something totally different and energetic, in order to refocus on your life in the ordinary world.

RITUAL TAROT
Making a ritual of a reading might prove helpful to some people. You could burn incense, light a candle, and keep your cards wrapped in neutral black silk in a wooden box.

THE WHOLE PERSON
SPREAD

THIS SPREAD USES ONLY THE MAJOR ARCANA AND GIVES
AN OVERALL PICTURE OF YOURSELF. IT IS MOST USEFUL
FOR DEEP MEDITATION ON YOUR LIFE AND THE
DIRECTION YOUR LIFE SHOULD BE TAKING.

The central card of the reading represents your innermost core, and the three other cards should each be interpreted in relation to this central card. On the left is your intellectual life, on the right your emotional life, and at the top your spiritual life. Ideally, these four cards should interact positively.

At the center of this Whole Person spread is the Star – a positive card to have in this central position because it symbolizes hope, renewal, and replenishment. To the left of the Star, the Wheel of Fortune, shown in this pack as the Wheel of Truth, shows that everything constantly turns in this querent's life. The overturning of old ways of thinking encourages new ideas, and this card interacts

well with the Star. To the right of the Star, the Empress shows the warmth of home, romance, and natural growth. All of these meanings would be well nurtured by the refreshing, replenishing nature of the Star.

Justice, placed above the Star, implies discernment between spiritual light and darkness. Perhaps the querent accepts all spiritual ideas and practices as equally valid. This card suggests a weighing of one against another, with the sword of truth and justice to separate right from wrong. The querent should use the positive ideas of the Star as a guide to find which spiritual paths are blessed with hope and inspiration and will lead to genuine renewal.

KASHMIR TAROT

Spiritual

Intellectual

Innermost core

Emotional

THE PROGRESSION
SPREAD

THIS STRAIGHTFORWARD SPREAD CONTAINS SIX CARDS.
IT SHOWS THE PATH FROM THE PRESENT TO THE
FUTURE AND THE WAY THAT THIS PATH COULD OR
SHOULD BE BROUGHT ABOUT.

The Progression spread has two cards that represent each position, and the meaning of each position is dependent on how the two cards interact with each other.

The querent provided some background information to assist the Tarot reader. The querent is a musician and wants to find out how her band can become much more successful.

During this reading, the querent complained that her band was not getting the success that she felt it deserved, and asked how she could improve the band's situation. The first two cards to be placed, the Star and Judgment in the present position, show that the

CELTIC TAROT

Present

querent should try to evaluate the band's past efforts and achievements with honesty (the Judgment card), in readiness for eventual rebirth, while the positivity of the Star card indicates that this should prove to be a process of hope, rather than negativity.

The next two cards to be placed, the Four of Swords and the Ace of Swords in the future position, show a period of recuperation and rest, and a break from troubles (the Four of Swords). The Ace of Swords suggests that the querent should be in a position to sit work (the Page of Coins), and there is a possibility of accepting advice or entering into negotiations with a professional involved with the arts (the King of Cups).

～◎～

Overall, this Progression Spread reading suggests that the querent's best course of

Path from present to future

Future

back and think clearly, rather than the card's other main meaning of strife and loss.

～◎～

The final two cards to be placed, the Page of Coins and King of Cups, show the path from the present to the future. The path is likely to involve meticulous, diligent action is to begin a thorough and careful rethinking of what the band is doing, engage in serious discussions with professionals in the music business, and take a complete break from the pressures of work in order to contemplate the various options of where to go next.

THE STAR
SPREAD I

EITHER THE MAJOR ARCANA OR THE WHOLE PACK CAN
BE USED IN THE STAR SPREAD WITHOUT AFFECTING
THE ORDER OF THE LAYOUT OR THE MEANINGS OF THE
POSITIONS. HERE, THE MAJOR ARCANA IS USED.

The central card is the heart of either the problem or the solution. The bottom card is your present position; above and to the left and right are your intellect and emotions; above them your known desires and what is yet to unfold; and at the top is the outcome. A very serious question is being asked; therefore, only the Major Arcana is used.

~⊙~

The querent wants to know how he can find a fulfilling love life. The Moon card at the heart of the spread shows confusion and deception. In the present position is the Fool – the querent – who is searching for a path through uncertainty. He wonders if he should stop intellectualizing his love life (the Hanged Man), and rely on his

emotions to make the difficult choices (the Lover). His conscious desires need to be overturned, and his pride needs to be knocked down (the Tower). The Chariot shows that when what is yet to unfold becomes apparent – perhaps hidden desires or a future relationship – he must retain a sense of balance. The outcome seems positive, with the Magician card showing control of the situation.

~⊙~

The Lover card in the emotions position suggests that the querent should consider the card's two meanings – choice and love. He is more likely to find a fulfilling love life if he chooses to allow his emotions to rule his heart than if he relies on his intellect to analyze his love life.

El Gran Tarot
Esoterico

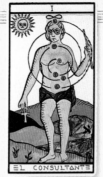

Outcome

Known desires

Heart of the question

What is yet to unfold

51

Intellect

Emotions

Present

THE STAR
SPREAD II

THIS SPREAD IS PARTICULARLY USEFUL IF YOU ARE
EXPERIENCING CONFLICT BETWEEN YOUR INTELLECT
AND EMOTIONS. IT CAN ALSO DIFFERENTIATE BETWEEN
KNOWN AND UNKNOWN DESIRES.

The querent wants to know whether she should continue writing novels – so far she has had no success in getting them published.

~ ⊙ ~

At the heart of this spread is the World card, representing completion and attainment. It is necessary to study the rest of the spread to discover whether this will be the final outcome or simply what the querent wants to happen.

~ ⊙ ~

The Four of Clubs in the present position suggests the fruits of hard work and creativity. In the intellect position, the Ace of Clubs is the essence of creativity and positive new beginnings. In the emotions position, the Queen of Cups is sensitive and intuitive, with an air of mystery. This augurs well for novel-writing, but also contains a warning to beware of being too unrealistic.

~ ⊙ ~

Illustrating known desires is Temperance, advising the querent to balance, perhaps, action and contemplation. That which is yet to unfold is Judgment, symbolizing honest evaluation, involving self-assessment and other people's judgments of the querent's efforts. The Emperor is in the outcome position and represents self-control and authority.

~ ⊙ ~

The answer to the question would seem to be yes – the querent should continue to write novels. This is made especially clear by the World card at the center of this spread, suggesting overall victory and success.

LE TAROT DE MARSEILLE

Outcome

Known desires

What is yet to unfold

Heart of the question

Intellect

Present

Emotions

THE HORSESHOE
SPREAD

THE SEVEN CARDS FOR THE HORSESHOE SPREAD ARE
LAID OUT IN ORDER FROM LEFT TO RIGHT. IT IS A
PARTICULARLY USEFUL SPREAD FOR SHOWING A PATH
FROM THE PAST TO THE FUTURE.

Moving from left to right, the first card represents the past, followed by the present, the future, the best course of action to take, the influence and effects of other people, obstacles that might be in the way, and finally, the outcome.

~ ୭ ~

The querent wants to know how he can earn more money. The Two of Cups suggests that the past has been good, with respect and support from others. The Five of Wands in the present position shows that any problems are simply minor annoyances, which he should easily be able to cope with. The Ten of Wands is a warning that too much success is a weighty burden, and he should consider if this is what he wants.

The best course card is the Ace of Swords, suggesting that the question requires clear thought. Other people around him are the real wealth (the Ace of Coins), perhaps financially, but mainly in themselves. The Ten of Cups in the obstacles position is a very positive card. It suggests that the querent is being offered a hard lesson, and if he wants to earn more money, it might have to be at the expense of deep personal fulfillment.

~ ୭ ~

The outcome shows that the querent can have his material success if he wants it, but the Queen of Coins suggests it might not be truly satisfying. The choice is the querent's, and perhaps his best course would be to think carefully and reassess his motivations.

Swiss IJJ Tarot

Past

Outcome

Present

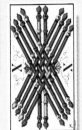

Future

Influence and effects

Obstacles

Best course

THE ALTERNATIVES
SPREAD

AS ITS NAME SUGGESTS, THIS IS AN EXCELLENT SPREAD
TO USE WHEN YOU HAVE TWO ALTERNATIVES – IT
SHOWS THE SAFE OPTION, AS WELL AS THE LESS
ORTHODOX AND MORE ADVENTUROUS OPTION.

In this spread, the top three cards represent the safer option, and the bottom three represent the riskier alternative. In each case the middle card is the focus, supported by the two flanking cards. The middle card is the first to be laid down and often illustrates the question, the problem, or even the solution.

~ ⊘ ~

The querent wonders if she should take the risk of going to France for a few months, or stay in the safety and security of her home. The middle card, the Knight of Swords, is intrepid and courageous, but sometimes impatient. The top three cards strongly suggest that the material security of home could easily be stagnation (the Four of Pentacles) in

which the querent feels trapped (the Eight of Swords). The Death card shows it is necessary to leave the past behind in order to make a fresh start.

~ ⊘ ~

The bottom three cards show the move to France. The King of Swords suggests that the move is not an easy option – he exercises firm judgment, but likes new ideas. The two flanking cards support these points – the Nine of Wands suggests determination to overcome obstacles, while the Six of Wands indicates success.

~ ⊘ ~

Clearly, the cards point toward a move to France by suggesting the abandonment of the past in favor of a riskier but ultimately more fulfilling future.

The safe option

MORGAN-GREER
TAROT

Summary of
the situation

The adventurous option

THE CELTIC CROSS
SPREAD

THIS REMARKABLY VERSATILE SPREAD CAN BE USED
FOR GENERAL OR SPECIFIC QUERIES, TO SHOW PAST,
PRESENT, AND FUTURE EVENTS AND INFLUENCES OR, AS
IN THIS CASE, TO PROVIDE AN OVERVIEW OF YOUR LIFE.

In this reading, Temperance in the present position shows balance and harmony. The King of Pentacles, solid, but too self-content, overlays it as an obstacle. Perhaps it represents a specific person or the querent's own lack of imagination. In the past he has tried hard to hold opposing forces in balance (the Chariot) and perhaps hang onto dreams and fantasies (the Moon). The future shows him cutting through this muddle (Ace of Swords), then skillfully balancing the variables in his life (the Two of Pentacles).

～◎～

Of the last four cards, the first, the Six of Swords, shows what the querent can do to influence events or the people around him. This card shows him overcoming obstacles and moving away from his present difficulties on a spiritual or physical journey. Strength encourages him to continue on this path. In the hopes and fears position, the King of Swords exercises authority, but also favors new ideas. With the progress implied by the Ace and the Six of Swords, and the versatility of the Two of Pentacles, the querent should certainly be able to reach a favorable outcome. The Three of Cups denotes peace and happiness, and reflects the harmony of the Temperance card.

～◎～

Balance and imbalance are recurrent themes in this reading, and the querent needs to stay rooted in the ideas of Temperance to ensure a successful outcome.

RIDER-WAITE TAROT

Outcome

Future influences

Hopes and fears

Past events

Obstacles/Present

Future events

How the world affects you

How you affect the world

Past influences

INDEX

ACKNOWLEDGMENTS

Artwork
Anna Benjamin

Special Photography
Steve Gorton and Sarah Ashun.
Thank you to the British Museum.

Editorial assistance Martha Swift,
Picture research assistance Ingrid Nilsson,
DTP design assistance Daniel McCarthy.

The publisher would like to thank the following for their
kind permission to reproduce material:

R. Armin: *The Original Tarot of Frown Strong* (1991); **Bear & Co.**, P.O. Box 2860,
Santa Fe, NM 87504: *Inner Child Cards*, by Mark Lerner and Isha Lerner, illustrations
by Christoper Guilfoil, Copyright 1992; **Nicolaas C. J. van Beek**, Amstelveenseweg
1090, 1081 JV Amsterdam, Netherlands: *Kashmir Tarot* (1984); **Editions Dusserre**,
4 Rue Nansouty, 75014 Paris, France: *Épitre aux Dames*; **Fireside**, Simon & Schuster
Inc., Simon & Schuster Building, Rockefeller Center, 1230 Avenue of the Americas,
New York, NY 10020, USA: *Mythic Tarot Deck* (Tricia Newell 1986); **Il Meneghello di
Osvaldo Menegazzi**, Via Fara 15, Milan, Italy: *Le Conchiglie Divinatore, Le Mani
Divinatore, Sardinia Tarot*; **Medea Advertising & Information Agency**, 143200
Y. Mozhaysk, Ul. Strelkovaya, D. 26, Russia: *Russian Tarot*; **Naipes Heraclio Fournier**,
P.O. Box 94, Vitoria, Spain: *El Gran Tarot Esoterico, Le Tarot de Marseille, Spanish Tarot*;
Cynthia Parzych Publishing Inc., 648 Broadway, New York, NY 10012 USA:
Elemental Tarot; **Piatnik**, Hutteldorse Strasse, Vienna, Austria: *Le Jeu du Destin Antique,
Celtic Tarot, Tarot de Marseille*; **Rider**, Random House UK Ltd, 20 Vauxhall Bridge
Road, London SW1V 2SA: *The Original Rider-Waite Tarot Deck*; **U.S. Games Systems,
Inc.**, Stamford, CT 06902 USA: *Haindl Tarot Deck* © 1990 by U.S. Games Systems,
Inc., *Medieval Scapini Tarot Deck* © 1985 by U.S. Games Systems, Inc., *Morgan-Greer
Tarot Deck* © 1979 by U.S. Games Systems, Inc., *Motherpeace Round Tarot* © 1981,
1983 by Motherpeace, Inc., *Pierpont Morgan-Bergamo Viscont-Sforza Tarocchi Deck* ©
1975, 1984 by U.S. Games Systems, Inc., *Rider-Waite™ Tarot Deck* © 1971 by
U.S. Games Systems, Inc., *Swiss IJJ Tarot Cards* © 1974 by U.S. Games Systems Inc.,
Tarot of the Witches © 1974 by U.S. Games Systems, Inc., *Ukiyoe Tarot Deck* © 1982 by
Stuart R. Kaplan, *Wonderland Tarot Deck* © 1989 by U.S. Games Systems, Inc.